HOW TO STOP OVERTHINKING

A Step-By-Step Guide to Reduce Stress, Overcome Anxiety with Courage and Poise, Rewire Your Anxious Brain, and Develop an Action-Oriented Mindset.

PRADIP N DAS

Table of Contents

Introduction

I came across a famous German story narrated by Sigmund Freud, the father of Psycho-Analysis. It happened once in a big hotel where a man came to stay. The manager was a little hesitant in giving him a room, although there was an empty room.

The man said, "Why are you hesitating so much?"

The manager said, "The reason is that a politician is staying just below that room, a very famous man and very powerful, a big gun. And he is annoyed by small things, so we have kept the room above him empty for three days since he has been here -- because if anybody walks, some noise is created. If you move something, some noise is created, and he becomes so irritated and so angry that he creates much fuss about it."

The stranger said, "Don't be worried! I will be cautious. Moreover, I am going to stay only overnight. I will be coming near about midnight because I have a lot of work to do in the town, and I will be leaving early in the morning, at five o'clock. There is not much possibility that I will do anything that will irritate the great man between twelve and five. I will be asleep and dreaming at most, and I don't think my dreams will disturb him."

The manager was convinced: "If he is going to stay just for five hours, there is no problem."

He was allowed.

At twelve, the man reached his room exhausted; the whole day's work, a thousand and one things clamoring in his head. He had forgotten entirely about the politician. He entered his room. He was so tired. He sat on his bed, took off one of his shoes, and threw it in the corner of the room. Then suddenly, the noise of the shoe reminded him that maybe the politician, the great leader, would get disturbed and may be awakened. So the other shoe he put down very silently.

After one hour, the politician knocked on his door. The man came out of his sleep, opened the door, and said, "Have I done anything? -- because for one hour, I have been asleep."

The politician was red with anger.

He said, "Yes! Where is the other shoe? I cannot manage to sleep. That other shoe goes on hanging, a continuous question in my mind -- where has the other shoe gone? Is this man sleeping with one shoe on? One I know you have thrown, but what happened to the other one? I have tried in every possible way to get rid of the idea -- that this is not my concern. How am I concerned with his shoe? But the more I have tried to get rid of the idea, the more I have become possessed by it. Now there is only one possible way to go to sleep: to come and wake you and ask you what happened. Unless I know, I cannot sleep."

Repeatedly thinking the same thing is overthinking. In other words, when you dwell or worry about the same thought repeatedly. People who overthink struggle to make decisions or take action. Overthinking can contribute to — depression, anxiety, health issues, unhappiness, poor performance, relationship issues, etc.

Usually, overthinking falls into two categories: ruminating about the past or worrying about the future.

If you're struggling with overthinking, you may feel "stuck" or unable to take any action at all. It can be hard to get the thoughts out of your mind or focus on anything else in the present.

Overthinking is thinking too much. When you overthink, you are overthinking instead of acting and doing things.

When you analyze, comment, and repeatedly repeat the same thoughts; you are overthinking instead of acting. This kind of thinking wastes your time and energy and prevents you from acting, doing new things, and making progress in your life.

Overthinking – The reasons

"Overthinking" is something of a misnomer. It is not really referring to thinking "too much," but instead to thinking unproductively about things that can neither be predicted nor controlled. Overthinking is a pattern in which your thoughts and worries circle in an endless loop. Instead of preparing you for the next steps, overthinking usually leads to inaction because you're overwhelmed by fear. Overthinking can be an early indicator of depression, anxiety, and other mental health conditions.

An over-thinker can easily confirm how the progression of overthinking makes you suffocate and exhausted and how all that thinking was an absolute waste at the end of the day. Overthinking is characterized as unproductive and can further lead to rumination. It makes it difficult to enjoy daily activities and disrupts our emotional regulation and sleep patterns.

These days overthinking diverse life circumstances and other easy-going things is an across-the-board issue. It does not imply that instructing yourself or thinking over your issues is something awful; however, on the off chance that you have a propensity to bend everything around in your mind until you see it in each point and plausibility, at that point, you are an over-thinker. Thinking over different things and occasions is a characteristic of life for some individuals. It, as a rule, causes individuals to discover arrangements of their issues and prepares them to confront life's challenges and overcome obstructions.

An incredible assortment of focal points and disservices of being an over-thinker is incredible. Do you prefer to know the reasons why those irritating considerations about different issues cause you to overthink? Peruse on to discover a couple of irrefutable reasons why you overthink your issues.

Stress and Anxiety

The main factors that can lead to overthinking are Stress and Anxiety. Apart from these basics, issues with one's self-esteem and self-doubt are other common causes of overthinking. We are fearful of your future- uncertainty about everything, such as illnesses, deaths, and finances. These situations have led us to the path of overthinking.

Uncertainty

The absence of certainty is one of the primary things that cause overthinking. When you dither about things you do, you let vulnerability and dread fill your brain. No one can tell where your choices will lead you; that is why you should go out on a limb without tormenting yourself. When you begin making choices, you will consequently help your certainty. When you are certain and solid, you will overcome all troubles without making a decent attempt.

Fear

Another trap that people fall into many times is that they are lost in vague fears about a situation in their lives. The best thing to get over such a situation is by asking themselves, what is the worst that could happen?

And when they have figured out the worst that could happen, they can also spend a little time thinking about what they can do if that often pretty unlikely thing happens.

Trauma

Trauma causes overthinking. People who have experienced trauma are more vulnerable to overthinking. For example, childhood abuse or parental neglect can alter an individual's brain to stick in a constant hyper-vigilance state. That is to say, our response of fight or flight or freeze in danger situations is on high alert. Therefore, in such conditions, people with trauma may experience obsessive thoughts.

The worst that could realistically happen is usually something that is not as scary as what people's minds running wild with vague fear could produce.

Finding clarity in this way usually only takes a few minutes and a bit of energy, and it can save you a lot of time and suffering.

Perfectionist

Perfection is an illusion. Nobody is perfect, and nothing is perfect. Perfection is the process of improvement. Those people who hold perfectionist values or have obsessive tendencies and those who are strict on gaining control may find themselves overthinking quickly. Such individuals begin to ruminate about their past mistakes or the ones they may make. They tend to worry about the judgments of others around them.

Overthinking and perfectionism go hand in hand. Perfectionists tend to fall into the trap of overthinking to the point where they don't accomplish anything. Here's the thing... being a perfectionist isn't about wanting things to be perfect. Instead, it's about thinking that things need to be perfect. Do you see the distinction?

As a recovering perfectionist, I know how challenging it can be to do a "good enough" job. My inner expectations used to be wildly unrealistic. If something wasn't done perfectly, it meant that it was bad. Don't get me wrong. There is nothing wrong with working hard. However, there comes the point when overachievement kicks in, and you start to lose yourself. I hate to break it to you, but perfect doesn't even exist. Hence, there is no point in trying to be perfect.

Re-thinking

It is wiser to settle on choices all the more effectively and rapidly. You should simply dispose of the propensity to re-think yourself. Re-thinking makes you audit the circumstance repeatedly in your brain since you have a hunch that you have not done things appropriately. Subsequently, you are forever discontent or substance that you have settled on the correct decision. Attempt to be progressively sure about yourself and in your capacities. It will enable you to be less fixated on your easy-going choices as the day progresses.

Undo button is absent

The journey of life cannot be unwinding. People don't want to be faltered, so ultimately, keep on thinking. It frequently turns out that you cannot get your psyche off the issue you cannot quit thinking about.

Numerous delicate individuals live in consistent strain since they do not have the foggiest idea of how to unwind and supplant the chain of negative musings with positive ones.

The ideal way to divert yourself from overthinking is to practice or do yoga. Yoga is an ideal apparatus to quiet your rich creative mind down and alleviate your stress over the issue. Just sit and envision a glad spot that makes you feel confident, free, and fulfilled.

Signs of Overthinking

Overthinking has turned into a worldwide plague, as we live in confusing occasions that require such a tremendous amount of mental ability from us. Obligations, funds, passionate injury, and different issues leave our brains in a condition of overdrive. Through broad research, youthful and moderately aged grown-ups mainly play a part in overthinking. Following are the significant symptoms of overthinking;

Overanalyzing

Over-thinkers have one fundamental issue: they have a need to control everything. They need to plan out the future, but since they cannot anticipate it, this causes them extraordinary tension. They do not care about managing anything they cannot control. They have a noteworthy dread of the obscure, which makes them sit and think about every one of the alternatives as opposed to making a move. Truth be told, overthinking prompts poor basic leadership and decisions.

When you get yourself overthinking, attempt to take yourself back to the present minute through full breaths and think about something that loosens you. Attempt to consider how these contemplations will serve you right now, and this by itself ought to dispose of them, as you will see that they do not do anything for you yet motivate incredible pressure.

Stiffen up of muscles and joints

Overthinking affects your muscle, joints, and other parts of your body. If your body is affected, it moves to your emotional aspect. You will continuously experience sorrow and pain unless the main culprit is addressed. Overthinking kicks off in our brain, but it has an impact on our physical and emotional aspects, leaving us feeling sluggish and exhausted.

In general, you need to concentrate on doing things that you enjoy and motivate yourself to stay active. You can enroll in a workout program and connect with positive people. You can also eat nutritious foods and practice mindfulness, and perhaps the most vital thing is knowing how to accept reality. You also need to know how to develop a positive rapport with yourself. View your thoughts as a tool to learn new things in life, not a factor that affects your progress.

Experiencing headaches

While you are experiencing regular migraines, you do think most likely excessively. Migraines sign to our bodies that we need a break, and this incorporates a rest from our own personalities. Additionally, if you give close consideration to your musings, you likely consider very similar things over.

Worriers will, in general, have negative idea designs that kept running in a circle, so as to battle this, attempt to fortify positive contemplations. Invest energy in your breathing and concentrating on care, and you should see the cerebral pains leave in a matter of moments.

In case you are experiencing constant headaches, you perhaps overanalyze things. A headache is an indication that your mind and body need rest. If you pay attention to your thinking, perhaps you think about similar matters time and again.

Being fearful

Research conducted by Nolen-Hoeksema discovered that fear causes you to resort to drinking alcohol, smoking, and drugs to drown your bad thoughts.

If you experience this symptom, you must try meditation or any techniques which encourage mindfulness. Allow ten to twenty minutes a day to get your worries out; it doesn't matter if it is through talking to your friends or singing. In this way, you can go on with your day and get rid of your worries.

You overanalyze things. The main issue of overthinkers is that they need to handle everything. They need to reform the future; however, because they are not able to forecast it, it leads them to feel stress and sadness. Overthinkers don't want to deal with anything they are not able to control. They have so much fear of the identified that it causes them to mull over the choices rather than do things to address the issue.

Overthinking also leads to poor judgments and decision-making.

Also, overthinkers have a never-ending desire for excellence in everything they do. They aren't able to accept failure. They do the whole thing in their ruling to keep away from it. Ironically, usually, this consists of doing nothing. Keep in mind; that fear can paralyze overthinkers. Therefore, rather than risking failure, they did not put themselves in a situation to not succeed at all.

Suppose this sounds like you; recollect that you are far beyond your mix-ups and disappointments. Additionally, remember that you need to commit a few errors to go anyplace throughout everyday life. These enable you to develop, learn, and achieve new statures in your advancement.

Failure to stay in the present moment

In the event that you cannot remain right now and appreciate life as it comes, at that point, you are a casualty of overthinking. Excessive thinking makes you lose the focal point of your general surroundings and become caught in your psyche. Getting to be stalled with considerations expels you from the now and can upset your associations with others.

Make sure to open your psyche and heart to your general surroundings and avoid getting so enveloped with negative thinking. Just permit contemplations into your cerebrum that serve your prosperity, and attempt to disregard those that just cut you down. Life offers so much excellence and the open door for fantastic encounters, yet you can possibly welcome this in the event that you figure out how to block it out of your mind and into your heart.

Likewise, associations with others help to quiet those negative musings. When we focus on others, we offer ourselves a reprieve and, along these lines, put our attention on another person. Figure out how to really tune in to other people, bond with them, and ask them inquiries about their lives. We can stop this endless overthinking issue together by shaping networks once more and figuring out how to help and associate with each other.

Center around doing things that make you feel better and urge you to stay dynamic. Begin an activity program, join gatherings to interface with similarly invested individuals in your locale, eat well nourishments, have a care practice, and figure out how to develop a positive association with yourself. Take a gander at your considerations as instruments to enable you to develop, not as adversaries that ruin your advancement.

Always in doubt

In order to achieve flawlessness, over-thinkers continually break down, reanalyze, and reinvestigate any circumstance. They would prefer not to settle on the off-base choice, so they set aside a long effort to settle on any decision since they do not confide in themselves. They are withdrawn from their instinct, so every choice originates from the mind, and this is not generally something to be thankful for. On the off chance that the mind is so foggy and hindered that you cannot settle on a reasonable choice, at that point, you are indeed an over-thinker.

Figure out how to confide in your instinct and go with your gut. In the event that notably, contrarily, in any event, you will have gained from experience and have more life exercises added to your repertoire.

Overthinkers continuously examine and re-examine any situation due to the aspiration for perfection. They are afraid of creating the wrong choice. Therefore, they take a lot of time in decision making, as they don't have confidence in their choices. Overthinkers are also out of touch with their instinct. Therefore, each choice comes from their brain, which is not good. If your brain is bogged down and very foggy, you cannot make a good choice; then you are indeed an overthinker.

You can address this by learning how to have confidence in your instinct. If you made a wrong decision cheer up, the most important thing is you acquired a lesson from your mistake.

Insomnia

Often insomnia and overthinking go hand-in-hand. So people with insomnia commonly try to shut out thoughts that stop them from sleeping. This might sound sensible at first, but it can cause more problems than it solves.

Over-thinkers know the trouble of nodding off great. Sleep deprivation takes a hang on you since you cannot close off your cerebrum. Your mind races, and you feel too tired even to consider sleeping; every one of the stresses from the day continues flooding your brain, and you cannot escape from this psychological jail.

Insomnia may strike you since you aren't able to shut off your brain, and your thoughts paralyze you bit by bit. Your thoughts race, and you feel very restless to sleep. The worries keep on lingering in your mind, and you cannot escape from this condition.

You could try repeating a word (articulatory suppression), doing a mental puzzle, or distracting yourself (articulatory suppression). You can do yoga, writing, drawing, composing, read, meditating, or converse with a friend or family member before going to sleep. Do things that remove the bad thoughts from your mind. Accomplish something that removes the move from your considerations and onto something different that enables your imagination and feelings to rise to the top.

Get Exhausted easily

When we feel tired routinely, this requires an activity plan on our part. Our bodies need us to tune in and tune in to their sign, rather than continually starting with one movement and then onto the next and disregarding its calls. While weakness can likewise be brought about by working excessively and not resting, overthinking can likewise cause weariness. When you consider different things troubling you too frequently, you do not give your mind a rest. Your psyche cannot run all day; you will get worn out in the long run.

We did not have much to stress over when we lived out in nature, so we had less to consider. In the advanced world, we have chaotic lives that expect us to do as much in such a brief period, but we have significantly, even more a need to back off and focus on our prosperity. On the off chance that you feel exhausted, back off and make sense of what your body and mind need from you.

Threats of Overthinking

Thinking has both negative and positive sides. If you think you get a solution. If you overthink, you get questions. And that leads to many more questions. For human beings, anything that costs your mental instability is a threat. Because of overthinking, we lose our peace, get anxious, and feel sad and depressed. We tend to make unreal assumptions.

When you are overthinking, your mind tirelessly goes on producing continuous unending thoughts, analyzing people, situation and negatively judging yourself. Overthinking has many threats in life, and therefore, it is crucial to work on eradicating this problem. It is not actually a mental disorder, but it can augment your chances of getting into it.

Too much thinking can affect the daily diet, sleep, and relationships with the family and friends and adversely affect the life. Too much concern can adversely impact lifestyle habits and performance in the workplace. A lot of people who overthink are stress-ridden; they look for respite in harmful lifestyle routines like cigarette smoking, overeating, taking drugs, and drinking too much.

While many people find themselves overthinking for the first time, others might have had a lingering problem. According to experts, overthinking is like a hamster wheel; as one hamster gets off, another takes its position, and the wheel goes on spinning.

It's likely that overthinking causes mental health to decline, and as your mental health declines, you are more likely to overthink. It's a vicious downward spiral.

Kills productivity

Continuing thoughts longer time starts affecting daily life. It can result in loss of sleep and appetite, slow reaction time, missing the present moments and opportunities, and problems in relationships and the workplace. The real problem starts when it begins to affect daily functioning.

If you are thinking all of the time, you are destined to fall into a negative cycle of rumination. I don't know about you, but repeatedly dwelling on the same thoughts is highly frustrating and counterproductive. Even worse, it can affect your emotional and mental well-being. Like anything else in life, thinking is helpful when used in moderation. Unfortunately, a lot of people have lost touch with their present reality because they are too in their heads.

Research has found that the average person has between 12,000 and 60,000 thoughts per day. Unfortunately, 80% of those thoughts are negative, and 95% are the same ones from the day before—your monkey mind's way of trying to take you away from the present moment. Everyone overthinks from time to time. However, chronic overthinkers are incapable of getting out of their heads. Not surprisingly, they struggle to get anything done because they are stuck in analysis paralysis.

Taking action starts with making a decision. The problem is that we live in a world where we are bombarded with choices, making a decision that much more difficult. Thanks to the Worldwide

Web, we have access to much information at our fingertips.

Overthinking isn't constructive as it's mainly negative. It leads to extreme decisions. It's a self-defeating pattern since it leads to time and energy loss and sabotages the willingness to work. You will also lose the "opportunity cost" involved, which means the time wasted over this destructive activity could have been otherwise utilized on something constructive.

Insomnia

You may have experienced that when you want to sleep, but your active mind prevents you from doing so. Your body might be tired, but your mind is wandering here and there.

When people force themselves to go to sleep, that will never work. Falling asleep is something that your mind cannot control. By overthinking about going to sleep or even other anxious thoughts in general, you will lose sleep quality, significantly affecting your mental and physical health.

Depression

Depression comes from thinking about your past repeatedly, making you very miserable. There are other causes of depression, like an illness or a disorder. Overthinking breeds fear and anxiety, which in turn can develop into depression.

Some people always carry their past experiences on their shoulders. The biggest lesson depressed people have to learn is that nobody can alter the past. The best way to get over this is to learn from our experiences and move on with a stronger and more knowledgeable mind. Just like anxiety, depression can also lead to suicidal thoughts or, even worse, suicide.

Anxiety

Overthinking and excessive worrying create feelings of distress and restlessness that may lead to anxiety or depression if left undealt with. Taking back control of your thoughts is the key to feeling peaceful again.

When we worry about the future, anxiety starts producing. Your thought creates emotions of fear, anger, happiness, or excitement. Highly anxious people are, in fact, overthinkers. They create so many scenarios on what is going to happen in their brains about their future. It is easy to be overwhelmed with negative emotions like fear, worry, and stress by overthinking a certain matter.

Normal worry doesn't get in the way of your daily activities and responsibilities. But worry becomes excessive when it's persistent, uncontrollable, and gets in the way of life. While everyone overthinks certain situations once in a while, chronic over-thinkers spend most of their waking time ruminating, putting pressure on themselves. They then mistake that pressure to be stress.

Worry is very much mentally exhaustive. It prevents you from being in the present moment. Too much anxiety can make you miserable; therefore, you will feel exhausted and sometimes depressed because your life is being caged in your emotions that were created by your thoughts. Even worse, anxiety can also lead to suicidal tendencies.

These thoughts are energy-draining and distressing. They could happen to anyone under stress. But when you reach the point where your thoughts and worrying prevent you from doing what you want to do — from living your life to the fullest — you should take action.

Kills happiness

Overthinking not just kill your happiness; sometimes, it leads to problems that don't even exist in the first place. It consumes all your focus and attention completely; it controls your body. There is no doubt in believing that the mind is the most powerful part of a body. After all, it is a hub of thoughts.

While thinking deeply about a topic can aid your professional life, overthinking can potentially squash your productivity, stifle your creativity, and exhaust your problem-solving capabilities. The result? A loss of happiness.

People who overthink generally do that about the past. They can't seem to let go. And happiness is a state of mind that you must continue to feed positive images and thoughts to. Generally, those who overthink are too encased in a negative pod of their own, excluding the present.

Thus, overthinking about what happened before usually prevents you from enjoying the happiness of what is happening now and after.

Paralysis

Overthinking can lead you to be unable to make decisions and lead you to nowhere. Maybe you have thought of a thousand ways a thing could go right or wrong, but you are afraid to make the decision just in case something goes wrong.

This may happen when you are starting a business, a restaurant, planning to marry a girlfriend, or doing a course for skill development. You keep overthinking, and it prevents you from actually taking any actions.

Yes, she may say no, yes, your business might fail, and yes, your restaurant may not be successful, or you may not acquire the skill you desire. It is like shooting a basketball; if you don't shoot, there's zero chance that you can make it, but if you shoot, you will more likely be succeeded.

Solutions for Overthinking

Jane is a good-hearted girl. She spends a lot of time with friends, goes to watch movies, and eats out at restaurants. Before she watches a movie with her friends, they spend an hour deciding what they are going to watch. Sometimes, they change their decision altogether and watch something else when they actually get there. While in the movie, she is worried that they should have seen the first movie they picked.

After the movie, Jane and her friends go to eat at a pizza shop. They all order pizza, but Jane is worried that she isn't going to pick the one that tastes the best.

She struggles to make a choice, and by the time the waitress arrives, she doesn't know what to pick. She finally makes a decision but regrets it, thinking that she could have picked something better.

That night, when Jane returned home, she complained to her mom that she didn't see the movie she thought she wanted to and wished she had a better pizza.

Jane's mom looked at her and said, "Well did you have fun with your friends at least?" Jane thought about it for a moment.

She couldn't remember; she was too focused on making meaningless decisions into big problems.

Time is fleeting, and moments are fleeting. You live in the past and away from the present by overthinking everything.

Make a decision and stick to it. Just let go. Forget about it. If the pizza you chose is tasteless, let it be tasteless. Order a different one next time and laugh about it with your friends.

It takes practice, but if you can learn to let go and realize that overthinking everything is meaningless in the great picture of your life, you will have much better memories of the good times and the places you go.

Turn bad decisions into funny stories; you cannot make perfect decisions in life about anything, especially not by overthinking them in the first place.

When you overthink, thoughts move around your head, and you find yourself stuck, unable to move forward. More so, you start coming up with bizarre ideas that totally contradict each other.

"I'm so excited for this job interview" transforms into "I wonder if they liked me" and or "oh, I'm so stupid! I shouldn't have said that! I'm definitely not getting an offer."

You start blaming yourself for things you didn't do and worrying about scenarios that may or may not happen.

Overthinking is simply the act of "thinking about something too much or for too long."

At any given point in life, it is possible to direct our thoughts in such a way that changes our perception of the same set of circumstances from bright and sunny to dark and stormy. Take an example of the first relationship. One minute, we may be thinking, "I'm so excited about this guy." A moment later, the thought morphs into "I wonder why he hasn't called me yet. Was he not really into me?" And finally, as we slip down the slippery slope of overthinking, our mind floods with attacks like, "He was probably just a jerk anyway. No one will actually be interested in *you*. Why do you even try?"

The not-calling example is easy because most of us can relate in the early stages of a relationship to the chaotic tangle of thoughts that flood our minds, interpreting and over-analyzing, combing emails for tone, and decoding ambiguous emojis. Yet, the problem of overthinking extends into many areas of our lives. While time spent in reflection is an integral part of being a mindful, curious, and self-aware individual capable of growth and change, time lost in destructive rumination perpetuates a cycle of self-limiting and self-destructive thinking and behavior. So how can we learn when, where, and how to focus our attention? How can we stop the vicious cycle of overthinking?

Solution 1: Snapping Technique

It is a method based on scientific research. This technique really helped many and decreased their problem by a considerable amount.

Take a simple band and tie it on your wrist. When you feel you are overthinking or going deep down on thoughts, just snap the rubber band on your wrist. The harder you snap it, the more it will be of help. And then, after snapping, your brain gets alerted that you are overthinking.

Now that you are aware and know that you shouldn't overthink, just replace these thoughts with another one or concentrate on things happening then. You can also perform other tasks like reading a book or going for a walk.

Consulting a psychologist would be the terminal stage. If thought is killing you repeatedly, you can try switching tasks immediately, which can divert your mind.

Have you heard the saying, "Yesterday is history, tomorrow is a mystery, but today is a gift; hence it's called the present" most of us tend to live in the regret of the past or the imagination of the future but focus less on the present. When we dwell in the present, we think about what we see instead of what we saw.

Solution 2: Set Time Limits

An effective step an overthinker can take to overcome the negative effects of the habit is to go to the store and purchase a timer. They can also download a timer app on their phone. This method has proven the most effective for those who have struggled with conquering their habitual overthinking with more direct efforts in the past without any success or noticeable progress.

Many psychological habits have some of the same effects as addiction. Overthinking is one of those habits. Symptoms similar to those associated with withdrawal in addicts are something that overthinkers have had to experience when trying to stop their overthinking cold turkey through distractions or denial. These individuals focus all their mental and emotional energy on denying their thoughts or distracting themselves when negative overthinking takes over their minds. There is no positive effect associated with this type of denial, and it only serves to make the overthinking worse by making the habit and not caving to it all that they can think about. Obsessing about overthinking is just as damaging and dangerous to a person's mental, emotional, and physical health as habitual overthinking itself.

Instead of stopping overthinking, this method allows individuals to let their overthinking run throughout their minds, but on their terms and within their chosen time frame. The first step in this practice is to find a timer. Once that has been done, the person needs to decide how long they want to devote to their overthinking habit.

Solution 3: Increase activeness

One of the best practices for those looking to stop their habitual overthinking is getting the blood pumping and start moving. Overthinking tends to happen most frequently when people have nothing else to occupy their thoughts productively. During those downtimes, or when the person is looking for a distraction, people start to ruminate about past actions or possible issues they expect in the future. That is why most people report that the majority of their overthinking begins in places while they are waiting for their ride and becomes the most dominant in their thoughts around bedtime as they try to fall asleep.

One change people make when trying this method for overcoming their habitual overthinking is picking up a new habit! Preferably, this habit gets either the mind or the body active and distracted from repetitive, stressful thoughts that kick off the overthinking sessions. Increased blood flow, airflow, and muscle stretching are all physical benefits involved with most extracurricular activities, and they also have psychological benefits like improving focus and boosting positive energies.

Giving people something else to focus on, picking up a new habit, or starting a new routine is one of the most trusted and proven methods of beating overthinking habits and replacing them with something that carries its own benefits for any person's physical, emotional and mental health.

Solution 4: Increase your self-awareness

Self-awareness is very much essential to stop overthinking. For that, you need to learn to be aware of it when it's happening before addressing or coping with your habit of overthinking. Any time you find yourself doubting or feeling stressed or anxious, step back and look at the situation and how you're responding. At that moment, awareness is the seed of the change you want to make. The first step to putting an end to overthinking is to be more aware of your thoughts to increase your self-awareness, psychologically, emotionally, and mentally. The more self-aware someone is, the more control they will be able to maintain over their thoughts, actions, and behaviors in situations that put pressure on them. More self-aware people are also better able to live in the moment.

You can find the time to go inward and reflect. If it helps your process, write down your thoughts. If you notice that the majority of your thoughts are negative in nature, it's time to reprogram. The present moment is all you have, yet most people continue to ignore it.

I see too many people obsess about the future to the point where they forget what is happening here and now. As a result, they get stuck in their thinking minds. While you are reading this, be fully in this moment. Don't try to label anything. Just notice what you are aware of and what is coming up for you. As Steve Jobs once said, "If you just sit and observe, you will see how restless your mind is... If you try to calm it, it only makes things worse. However, over time it does calm, and when it does, there's room to hear more subtle things."

Solution 5: Change your thought pattern

Overthinking is a product of fear, and we soon begin to pay attention to all the negative things that might occur. However, once you master to sense you are overthinking, you can stop and continue to think about all the positives. Spend time thinking about the things that can go right. Or focus on something different. Immerse yourself in a hobby. For example, painting, reading, knitting, crafting – whatever takes your fancy.

One issue that most overthinkers struggle with is thinking about the past and replaying their words and actions or the inability to react through their mind. These overthinking sessions fill the person's mind with thoughts of what they should have said or done or that they should have walked away from something negative instead of getting involved and making the situation worse for themselves.

This is where overthinkers need to abandon their regrets, releasing them from their thoughts and trying to move forward on a more positive lifestyle path. Once they are willing to let go of these negative thoughts and emotions, they can be replaced with a more positive way of thinking that will help people break their overthinking habits and improve the way they see the world around them.

People who use gratitude to overcome their habitual overthinking start by making a list of everything in their life that they are grateful for. It could be the basics like their family, friends, and other loved ones or be related to the situation currently inspiring their overthinking habits like being grateful for their being employed when difficulties at work are causing stress and panic within their personal emotions and thoughts and behaviors. Once a person is able to see in writing or digitally on a phone or computer screen in front of them all the good and positive influences in their life that they are grateful for, it is easier to push away those negative repetitive thoughts that are most powerful during times of overthinking.

People who know why they should be grateful and what they have that they are grateful for, it is easier to take a more positive view of the world around them, be it at work or in their personal life. Some people recommend carrying their list in a jacket pocket, purse, or wallet. If the list was made virtually, keeping a screenshot or copy of it saved on their phone or tablet, anywhere that it is easily accessible, no matter where they are, has proven to be the most helpful and most recommended technique for achieving success with this method.

Solution 6: Embrace Positive Thoughts

Many times, overthinkers focus on the negative aspects of their tasks or situations and what can go wrong over what can go right or how the person can benefit. They get overwhelmed by issues that can arise, any bad factors, and variables that could disturb their plans or decision process. Actually, these negative thoughts are the most powerful fuel behind their habitual overthinking.

People who focus on positive thoughts are able to acknowledge and react reasonably to negative emotions that arise in their different interactions and responsibilities. These types of people are more energized, better at socializing, and typically more driven in their tasks because their mind is not burdened with stressful or painful thoughts that they are unable to break free from the repetition.

Solution 7: Schedule Thinking Time

Thinking is the process of considering ideas to make decisions, actions, and the like. It is a process of examining and weighing possible reactions and actions. This act is vital and essential before decision-making. It is not easy to control how, when, and what to think about, but this is very achievable through constant practice.

As crucial as thinking is, we still have to control what we think about, when we think, and how frequently we do it. Leaving our minds to choose our thinking times might not be as healthy as we will be thinking at random. We can prevent this by scheduling our thinking time to a more comfortable period and sticking to it.

The thinking process is more suitable during the day than at night. This is because our minds need rest, and the perfect time to rest the mind is at night, while we sleep. Therefore, instead of keeping the mind busy at night, use it to think and sort out certain problems during the day. This will help you to have a perfect night's rest. However, when it comes to fantasizing about something, the most suitable time to do this is at night and not during working hours when you need to concentrate.

Overthinking is a habit formed over time, and changing it can take a while. Scheduling thinking time is one of the actions you can take to move away from overthinking.

Solution 8: Accept that nobody can alter past or predict future

This is a hard fact that no one can alter the past or predict the future. One of the leading causes of overthinking in men and women worldwide is the fear of what is unknown and the fear of what cannot be predicted. Another is the loss of control that comes with obsessing over past events or encounters that, in hindsight, could have been handled or more to a person's personal satisfaction.

The first step to stopping overthinking and all of the negative effects that come with it is to understand that there are things that no one can see coming and that there will always be things we think could have been handled better or that we wish we could change, and then accept these thoughts as fact. Once these facts have been accepted, the sense of freedom that most people feel is enough to get them through their difficult times and move forward from getting their thoughts stuck in a repetitive cycle that becomes habitual overthinking. That freedom and the positive emotions that come with it help with motivation and staying on track when people hang on to those good feelings and call on them when situations become complicated or overwhelming.

Until these facts are understood and embraced, no one will be able to control their habitual overthinking successfully, like those concerned for others but have not been able to help because the person is unwilling to acknowledge that they have an issue. Without self-awareness, overthinkers will get lost in negative thought cycles and become victims of their dangerous and negative side effects.

Solution 9: Fix Decision Making Time

While many people get stuck, they overthink everything to the point where they are unable to make a decision. It's important to consider your options before following through on something carefully. However, too much overthinking can put you into a state of paralysis and indecisiveness. This only leaves you feeling mentally and emotionally drained. Indecision is the greatest thief of productivity. Any decision is better than no decision at all.

Give yourself a time limit for making decisions. Ask yourself, "How long do I think about something before I have to make a decision?" Keep in mind that some decisions are bigger than others, so don't be hard on yourself. By giving yourself less time to overthink everything, you will get more done and feel less stressed.

We make decisions every day, and some of the decisions are life-changing. Everything about us is because of our decision-making. The relationship, health, education, and everything that makes us who we are today are our capacity or incapacity to make decisions and the choices we have already made. It is unfortunate that many people still find it hard to make decisions. Even if everything else seems to be going well for us, we curl up when the chips are down and the time calls for it to make that judgment call. It just seems so hard to decide on something and stick to it.

Indecisive people are more likely to be controlled by their lives instead of the other way around. With no control over your life due to indecisiveness, you may not be as self-sufficient as you would like; thus, you need to learn to be decisive and take charge of your life. Every day, we live by many decisions we have to make, however minute or huge. That is what life is all about. Progress will be more attainable if we break down these huge decisions into little ones.

The best way to instigate your overthinking habit is to have a decision to make with a need to get it right and more than enough time to make it. The whole process of contemplating the best step to take, considering all your options while taking your time, is just an invitation to overthinking things. Setting a time limit for yourself is really the most effective way to curb that habit. It is advisable to set a limit on the span based on the severity or magnitude of the decision.

You have no chance of overthinking and enforcing action through your set time limit. This is relatively easy; simply start timing yourself to make a decision. Because of your consciousness of time, your analysis of the advantages and disadvantages of time will be more specific and concise. In fact, this technique is very easy and doable.

This is very much helpful for those who take too much time to make decisions. You can set the time as short as 1 minute, or as long as 5 minutes, or any number in between.

Solution 10: Practice Meditation

One proven tool that is incredibly effective in helping people choose their thoughts and stop overthinking is mindfulness. "Mindfulness is actually a way of connecting with your life, and it's something that doesn't involve a lot of energy," said mindfulness expert Dr. Jon Kabat-Zinn. "It involves a kind of cultivating attention in a particular way... It's paying attention, on purpose, in the present moment non-judgmentally as if your life depended on it."

For the overthinkers out there, mindfulness can be a life-saver. Learning to control or focus your attention can enhance an inner sense of calm and lead to increased self-awareness. With this awareness, you can better understand and take power over your behavior. "Attention is the faculty that allows us to navigate our lives in one way or another and to actually know what's happening or know that we don't know what's happening and find ways to be in a wiser relationship to things that are going on in our lives [rather] than being at the mercy, say, of our own emotional reactions and crazy thoughts and fears and so forth," said Dr. Kabat-Zinn.

Practicing mindfulness meditation can help you to know your thoughts and react more calmly to them without catastrophizing or allowing them to spiral out of control. Psychologist Dr. Donna Rockwell refers to the mind as often jumping around "like a monkey or a wild horse." She describes mindfulness as a way of coming to know your own mind. "When you're sitting in meditation, it's like you're watching a movie of all your thoughts, said Dr. Rockwell. "Over time, what happens is that you just come to know that movie so well, and it can no longer take you off your spot...They say thoughts are like passing clouds, and if we can come to observe them that way, they don't have control over us."

Meditation and being mindful have been shown to enhance complete psychological well-being. It improves memory, concentration, and emotional regulation and reduces stress. Being mindful is simply about being present in the moment. Being mindful allows you to acknowledge your thoughts are there, and you choose not to accept them and pay attention to something that pleases you. Also, practice makes you perfect, so making a habit of doing mindfulness meditation will improve how you handle your overthinking.

Meditation can actually help you focus your mind away from the things troubling you. In fact, guided meditation can help you reset your mind, thus leaving you unburdened and refreshed, ready for all the challenges that may come your way.

Meditation is different from mindfulness; the latter is a spur of the moment technique that you can use anywhere and anytime. In the purest sense, meditation should be practiced in a calm, quiet, and relaxing environment as much as possible.

Here are a couple of meditation techniques. Give them all a try and choose the one that you vibe the most with.

Breathing is one of the body's involuntary actions, meaning you do not really need to command your body to breathe; it just happens. However, you can turn your breathing into a form of meditation just by noticing every breath you take.

In focused breathing meditation, you take long, slow, deep breaths, breaths so deep that you fill your abdomen with air as well. To practice this form of meditation, you disengage your mind from all thoughts and focus all your attention on your breathing. This is especially helpful when you start noticing that your thoughts are starting to go out of your control.

However, this technique might not be appropriate for those suffering from respiratory ailments, like asthma and some heart ailments.

When you focus on slowing your breath down, you slow your heart, which helps to calm your mind. You can now reset your thinking pattern with a calm mind and begin afresh with a healthy thinking style. Begin by filling your lungs with air and holding it for several seconds. Then slowly exhale the air, and once you get the urge to inhale, take another deep breath. Keep repeating this until you are relaxed.

Solution 11: Challenge Your Thoughts

It's easy to get carried away with negative thoughts. So before you conclude that calling in sick is going to get you fired or that forgetting one deadline will cause you to become homeless, acknowledge that your thoughts may be exaggeratedly negative.

Remember that your emotions will interfere with your ability to look at situations objectively. Take a step back and look at the evidence. What evidence do you have that your thought is true? What evidence do you have that your thought isn't true?

You need first to retrain your brain to stop overthinking. There are many exercises and activities that you can use to alter your thinking pattern.

When you are on the verge of dropping into that deep whirlpool of infinite negative emotions, you can start getting rid of them entirely, and you can start by challenging your thoughts before they run out of control.

Suppose you feel as if your boss is constantly and intentionally ignoring you. You think that the reason is that you somehow messed up something and that he may fire you very soon. Usually, these kinds of thoughts cause your mind to overthink and cause you to lose sleep, thus causing you to not be as efficient at work, which therefore leads to you getting fired. In short, overthinking problems turns them into self-fulfilling prophecies.

On the other hand, if you just step back and analyze your thoughts before your overactive brain blows them way out of proportion, you can control them better. Next, think about what you could do to avoid getting fired, like increasing your productivity or maybe learning a new skill that can help you do your job better.

Solution 12: Declutter Your Environment

The environments affect us profoundly that are not always obvious and immediately felt. An employee who must perform their tasks in an uncomfortable environment will inevitably underperform compared to another employee in a comfortable, clean environment.

Clutter increases the opportunities for distraction. Clutter doesn't have just to be physical; it can also be digital – like too many files on your computer or too many applications on your mobile and too many tabs open on internet explorer. This digital form of clutter can affect your productivity and ability to focus on a task.

The decision to organize and declutter your life is not only empowering, but it can have an enormously positive effect on your wellbeing – leading to more mindfulness, reduced stress and anxiety, a better quality of life, and better focus. You'll be able to start curbing the habit of accumulating unnecessary clutter.

Every person has a different personality, style, way of working, and comfort level when it comes to working in the organization.

In an office environment, organize your working space and reduce to the bare minimum. You'll notice it's much easier to work productively when your setting is clean and organized.

Decluttering goes far beyond improving the aesthetics of your home or workspace. It's essential to both your physical and mental wellbeing.

Whether it's dirty dishes piling up in the sink or stacks of papers or files covering your desk, everyone is bound to experience the negative effects of clutter in their lives. The clutter in our physical spaces can adversely affect our mental health. As more things occupy our physical space, they find a way to seep into our minds and increase stress and anxiety.

When you clear the excess clutter out of your life, you will notice the positive effects it has on your mental state and overall wellness. Many studies have proven the psychological power of clearing out your space in various areas of your life. For your overall health and happiness, take the time to declutter your life and start seeing the positive changes that occur.

Look around your home or personal living space. How does the way it looks now make you feel? Does it make you feel sad? Overwhelmed? Sometimes our lack of organization can get out of hand when it starts to feel like we can't control it. It's always futile to try and address the external effects before dealing with the internal effects of overthinking stress, anxiety, or depression. If you don't address the thought process and bad habits, then even if you manage to clean up your space, there is a good chance it will start to look just like it did before within weeks or even days.

Keep in mind that this process applies mainly to those of us who need assistance with something that has come to be something of an overwhelming task. You may have no problem keeping your home organized and clean, which is excellent. For those of you who can be described this way, my advice would be to think about introducing another element into your home that cultivates relaxation and comfort. Perhaps a small plant you can give attention to throughout the week or a plaque with a motivational quote you can place on the wall where you will see it every day. Any small reminder you can give yourself each day as you progress on your journey can be a massive boost in confidence.

You will also need a bag for trash. Sometimes when we've developed negative emotions associated with attachment, it can feel painful to let go of things we've held on to for a long time. Think about your goals in decluttering your environment. Weigh the importance of this or that object against what you are trying to accomplish in your life. If the emotional reaction attached to that object fits into the hindrance category in your life journey, then you need to get rid of it. Maybe someone you know can keep it for you if you can't bring yourself to trash or donate something. But holding onto it is only going to continue to hold you back.

This is the process you will follow for the rest of your space. If it starts to get overwhelming, take a break. You don't have to do it all in one day. Keep reminding yourself of what a big and important step you are taking to improve your life.

Areas like the kitchen and bathroom may prove to be the most work. Remember to remove and organize items before trying to clean surfaces, as this will only frustrate you and lead to a suboptimal level of cleanliness. If you can afford it, you may consider having a professional cleaning service come in to clean just a few of the most challenging rooms of the house. If they are really bad, don't feel ashamed. Just make sure you've removed and trashed any items you need to be out of the way. Many services will offer great introductory rates for new customers and one-time services.

There are many options for disposing of the items you've recognized you don't need or use. You can find donation boxes at stores like Goodwill or Salvation Army. Maybe there is a church you can donate to if you have items like baby clothes or toys. Another option is to have a yard sale. Make a little cash for those items, and rest assured that someone else is going to get some good use out of them.

Solution 13: Change your daily routine

You make subtle changes to your daily routine and stick to them religiously. In the future, you will notice a drastic improvement when you reflect on where you are then versus where you are now.

Drink a glass of water first thing in the morning. It kick-starts your metabolism, resumes hydration, and gives you the energy to begin your day.

Make exercise a top priority. Block off at least an hour a day for some type of movement and work your other priorities around it.

Make time for a hobby. You should force yourself to pick something up that you can lose yourself in. You can spend your time learning some music, instruments, languages, or playing sports. It soothes your mind. Hobbies are a healthy distraction, ignite creativity and stress relief, and boost confidence. The beauty of having one is that you don't need to be proficient in the hobby; you simply enjoy it.

Solution 14: Face the Fear

"Look fear in the face, and it will cease to trouble you."

The fear can manifest in multiple forms - over analysis, over planning, procrastination, indecisiveness, perfectionism - they don't matter. What matters is to see that it is meant to protect you from one thing: failure...or the uncertainty of success.

Due to this, you try to think until you are sure of achieving success. But getting to that point of certainty is logically impossible. You never imagine and think of all possible event paths.

To get rid of your fear, you need to face your fear.

There is no other way to get rid of overthinking.

You will find your freedom once you fight out your

fears.

The only way to deal with fear is to act in the face

of it, which is bravery. Having courage is the

quality of being able to act despite fear.

There's no "magic bullet" to developing courage,

but it gets easier the more you do it because you

gain strength from your own acts of courage.

Final Words

Teddy Roosevelt said the following: "In any moment of decision, the best thing you can do is the right thing, the next best thing is the wrong thing, and the worst thing you can do is nothing." Overthinking can be devastating and change how you work with others and how you do things. It can significantly affect your personal life, social life, and work life too. Most importantly, overthinking may also cause emotional distress. To overcome this, you will need to make some changes in your perspective and constantly shrug away any thoughts that make you feel astray.

People who overthink continuously try to evaluate their actions, fearing that they might have said something wrong. The anxiety that ensues holds them back from moving ahead in life in a peaceful manner. Once identified, it becomes vital to take care of them, lest they overpower our abilities to have a balanced life.

This disorder might not seem all that serious to people who are not suffering from chronic overthinking. However, it is like being trapped in your own personal hell for those who are constantly suffering from overthinking day in and day out. Overthinking is like getting trapped in a tiny cage that your own mind fabricated, and that cage gets smaller the longer you stay inside it.

Since you have made it to this point of the book, you are now armed with the one thing you need to get better: knowledge. You get to know how to eradicate overthinking or ultimately minimize its effect on your life. You also learned how to snap yourself out of your funk if your mind starts to spiral out of control.

Mindfulness, again, is not a cure-all; however, it does help you manage your overthinking habit. You have learned how to identify when you are about to fall into the endless pit of despair made by your overthinking mind, and you also know how to drag yourself out of your funk.

Thank you again for reading this book. I hope that this was able to help you manage your overthinking mind before things get even worse.

The next step is to reaffirm every day that you are on your way to becoming a better, fuller you. Review how far you've come so far and be proud! As with anything, the key to success is consistency and determination. Believe in yourself and your ability to make the changes necessary to realize your goals. Once you've removed the clutter from your mind, you will turn overthinking into focused achieving every day. You may have heard many times over, "easier said than done." Well, you should be excited to learn how to do what you set your mind to do. You've wanted to make a change for a long time. Taking steps to make your goals come to fruition is something many people never achieve.

After taking a big step forward in my life at times like this, I begin to reflect on how far I've come. It is hard to appreciate your progress sometimes when you are in the heat of battle and struggling every day during the beginning, middle, or even near the end of your efforts. There is nothing better than stepping up onto that final rung and looking down to see those completed steps in your wake.

Remember when you were sitting at square one, unable to free yourself from the chains of overthinking? I know it well—I've been there myself. It takes a great deal of courage to stand up and say I'm ready to make a change. It saddens me that many people continue to overthink and overanalyze throughout their lives, missing out on the experiences and appreciation that a free mind can realize. It is easy to slip into the comfortable habits of mindless eating, checking a phone or tablet every few minutes, and going to bed later and later until your system is all out of sorts. Sometimes, it seems too easy to give in and let what's easy overshadow what's worth working for. You don't have to be a slave to overthinking, and maybe it's possible for you to take what you've learned and help change the lives around you.

Perhaps you know someone who seems to be struggling with overthinking, stressing out about everyday challenges, and stress just like you were at the beginning of your journey. Consider reaching out and sharing what you've learned. Nothing feels better than sharing new knowledge with someone who can use it to make the positive changes you've seen happen in yourself. Maybe it's a co-worker, a spouse, or a close friend. Many people from different walks of life will benefit from the changes laid out in this book, so why not share your story!

Finally, life is not rocket science. It's very simple, but our thoughts, emotions, and wants complicate life. I have seen joyous people living a simple life and have seen people complaining and even trying to end their life with all the comforts, luxury, and richness surrounding them. I hope you have taken lots of notes and will take action. Good luck!!!

Disclaimer

Although the publisher and the author have made every effort to ensure that the information in this book is correct, and while this publication is designed to provide accurate information regarding the subject matter covered, the publisher and the author assume no responsibility for errors, inaccuracies, omissions, or any other inconsistencies herein and hereby disclaim any liability to any party for any loss, damage, or disruption caused by errors or omissions, and whether such errors or omissions result from negligence, accident, or any other cause.

The ideas, procedures, and suggestions in this book are not intended as a substitute for consulting with an expert. Neither the author nor the publisher shall be liable or responsible for any loss or damage allegedly arising from any information or suggestion in this book.

COPYRIGHT © 2022 PRADIP N DAS

Gratitude

This book is dedicated to all Mentors and Gurus who taught and inspire me to become an Author.

I sincerely thank the Almighty for the continued blessing and all the readers for their love and appreciation.

Jn